Guest Book to Celebrate

_____

_____

Event Date

_____

THANK YOU FOR COMING.

Let's celebrate!

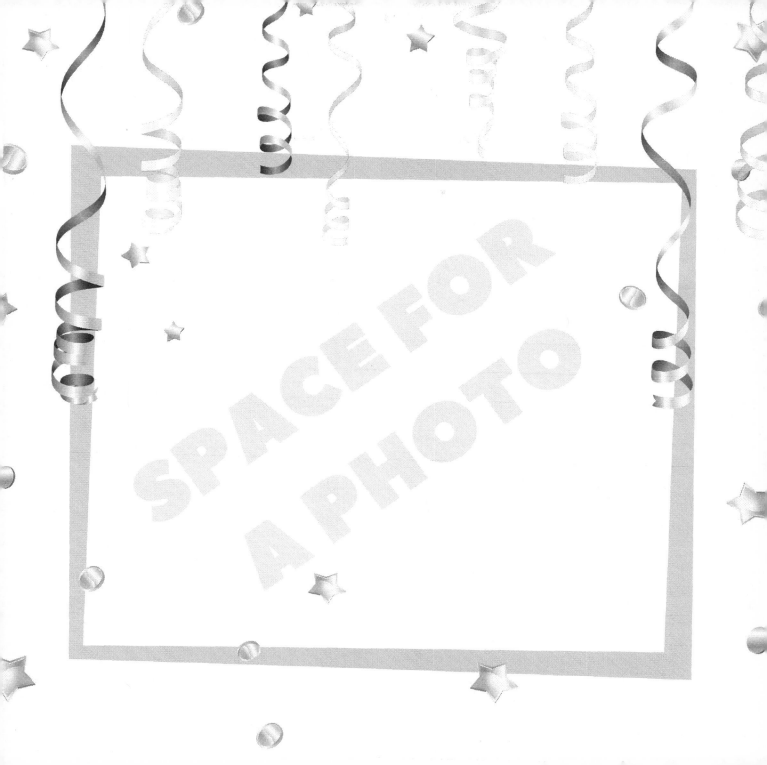

Guest Name

Thoughts & Messages

_____

_____

_____

_____

_____

_____

_____

EMAIL/PHONE

Guest Name

Thoughts & Messages

_____

_____

_____

_____

_____

_____

_____

EMAIL/PHONE

Guest Name

Thoughts & Messages

_____

_____

_____

_____

_____

_____

Email/Phone

Guest Name

_____

Thoughts & Messages

_____

_____

_____

_____

_____

_____

EMAIL/PHONE

Guest Name

Thoughts & Messages

EMAIL/PHONE

Guest Name

Thoughts & Messages

_____

_____

_____

_____

_____

_____

_____

EMAIL/PHONE

Guest Name

_____

Thoughts & Messages

_____

_____

_____

_____

_____

_____

EMAIL/PHONE

Guest Name

_____

Thoughts & Messages

_____

_____

_____

_____

_____

_____

_____

Email/Phone

Guest Name

_____

Thoughts & Messages

_____

_____

_____

_____

_____

_____

EMAIL/PHONE

Guest Name

_____

Thoughts & Messages

_____

_____

_____

_____

_____

_____

Email/Phone

Guest Name

_____

Thoughts & Messages

_____

_____

_____

_____

_____

_____

_____

EMAIL/PHONE

Guest Name

_____

Thoughts & Messages

_____

_____

_____

_____

_____

_____

_____

Email/Phone

Guest Name

Thoughts & Messages

_____

_____

_____

_____

_____

_____

_____

EMAIL/PHONE

Guest Name

_____

Thoughts & Messages

_____

_____

_____

_____

_____

_____

✉

EMAIL/PHONE

Guest Name

Thoughts & Messages

Email/Phone

Guest Name

Thoughts & Messages

_____

_____

_____

_____

_____

_____

Email/Phone

Guest Name

_____

Thoughts & Messages

_____

_____

_____

_____

_____

_____

_____

EMAIL/PHONE

Guest Name

Thoughts & Messages

Guest Name

_____

Thoughts & Messages

_____

_____

_____

_____

_____

_____

_____

EMAIL/PHONE

Guest Name

Thoughts & Messages

Guest Name

Thoughts & Messages

_____

_____

_____

_____

_____

_____

_____

Email/Phone

Guest Name

Thoughts & Messages

Guest Name

Thoughts & Messages

✉ Email/Phone

Guest Name

Thoughts & Messages

Guest Name

Thoughts & Messages

_____

_____

_____

_____

_____

_____

EMAIL/PHONE

Guest Name

Thoughts & Messages

Guest Name

Thoughts & Messages

Email/Phone

Guest Name

Thoughts & Messages

_____

_____

_____

_____

_____

_____

_____

Email/Phone

Guest Name

_____

Thoughts & Messages

_____

_____

_____

_____

_____

_____

EMAIL/PHONE

Guest Name

Thoughts & Messages

_____

_____

_____

_____

_____

_____

EMAIL/PHONE

Guest Name

Thoughts & Messages

Guest Name

Thoughts & Messages

_____

_____

_____

_____

_____

_____

_____

EMAIL/PHONE

Guest Name

Thoughts & Messages

_____

_____

_____

_____

_____

_____

_____

EMAIL/PHONE

Guest Name

Thoughts & Messages

Email/Phone

Guest Name

Thoughts & Messages

Guest Name

Thoughts & Messages

Email/Phone

Guest Name

Thoughts & Messages

_____

_____

_____

_____

_____

_____

_____

EMAIL/PHONE

Guest Name

Thoughts & Messages

_____

_____

_____

_____

_____

_____

_____

EMAIL/PHONE

Guest Name

Thoughts & Messages

EMAIL/PHONE

Guest Name

Thoughts & Messages

_____

_____

_____

_____

_____

_____

_____

Email/Phone

Guest Name

Thoughts & Messages

EMAIL/PHONE

Guest Name

Thoughts & Messages

_____

_____

_____

_____

_____

_____

_____

Guest Name

Thoughts & Messages

_____

_____

_____

_____

_____

_____

_____

EMAIL/PHONE

Guest Name

Thoughts & Messages

EMAIL/PHONE

Guest Name

Thoughts & Messages

Guest Name

_____

Thoughts & Messages

_____

_____

_____

_____

_____

_____

_____

EMAIL/PHONE

Guest Name

Thoughts & Messages

_____

_____

_____

_____

_____

_____

_____

Email/Phone

Guest Name

_____

Thoughts & Messages

_____

_____

_____

_____

_____

_____

_____

✉ E

Email/Phone

Guest Name

_____

Thoughts & Messages

_____

_____

_____

_____

_____

_____

_____

Email/Phone

Guest Name

Thoughts & Messages

Guest Name

Thoughts & Messages

Email/Phone

Guest Name

Thoughts & Messages

Email/Phone

Guest Name

Thoughts & Messages

Email/Phone

Guest Name

Thoughts & Messages

_____

_____

_____

_____

_____

_____

_____

EMAIL/PHONE

Guest Name

Thoughts & Messages

_____

_____

_____

_____

_____

_____

EMAIL/PHONE

Guest Name

Thoughts & Messages

_____

_____

_____

_____

_____

_____

_____

EMAIL/PHONE

Guest Name

Thoughts & Messages

_____

_____

_____

_____

_____

_____

_____

EMAIL/PHONE

Guest Name

Thoughts & Messages

_____

_____

_____

_____

_____

_____

_____

EMAIL/PHONE

Guest Name

Thoughts & Messages

_____

_____

_____

_____

_____

_____

_____

Email/Phone

Guest Name

Thoughts & Messages

Guest Name

Thoughts & Messages

Email/Phone

Guest Name

Thoughts & Messages

Guest Name

_____

Thoughts & Messages

_____

_____

_____

_____

_____

_____

_____

EMAIL/PHONE

Guest Name

_____

Thoughts & Messages

_____

_____

_____

_____

_____

_____

_____

EMAIL/PHONE

Guest Name

Thoughts & Messages

_____

_____

_____

_____

_____

_____

_____

Email/Phone

Guest Name

Thoughts & Messages

Email/Phone

Guest Name

Thoughts & Messages

EMAIL/PHONE

Guest Name

Thoughts & Messages

✉ E

Email/Phone

Guest Name

Thoughts & Messages

_____

_____

_____

_____

_____

_____

_____

EMAIL/PHONE

Guest Name

Thoughts & Messages

Email/Phone

Guest Name

Thoughts & Messages

✉ E

EMAIL/PHONE

Guest Name

Thoughts & Messages

Email/Phone

Guest Name

_____

Thoughts & Messages

_____

_____

_____

_____

_____

_____

EMAIL/PHONE

Guest Name

Thoughts & Messages

Guest Name

Thoughts & Messages

EMAIL/PHONE

Guest Name

Thoughts & Messages

_____

_____

_____

_____

_____

_____

_____

Guest Name

Thoughts & Messages

✉ Email/Phone

Guest Name

_____

Thoughts & Messages

_____

_____

_____

_____

_____

_____

EMAIL/PHONE

Guest Name

Thoughts & Messages

EMAIL/PHONE

Guest Name

_____

Thoughts & Messages

_____

_____

_____

_____

_____

_____

Email/Phone

Guest Name

Thoughts & Messages

✉ E

Email/Phone

Guest Name

Thoughts & Messages

Email/Phone

Guest Name

Thoughts & Messages

Guest Name

_____

Thoughts & Messages

_____

_____

_____

_____

_____

_____

_____

Email/Phone

Guest Name

Thoughts & Messages

Guest Name

Thoughts & Messages

Guest Name

_____

Thoughts & Messages

_____

_____

_____

_____

_____

_____

_____

✉ Email/Phone

Guest Name

Thoughts & Messages

Guest Name

Thoughts & Messages

EMAIL/PHONE

Guest Name

Thoughts & Messages

_____

_____

_____

_____

_____

_____

_____

Email/Phone

Guest Name

_____

Thoughts & Messages

_____

_____

_____

_____

_____

_____

Email/Phone

Guest Name

Thoughts & Messages

_____

_____

_____

_____

_____

_____

EMAIL/PHONE

Guest Name

Thoughts & Messages

Email/Phone

Guest Name

Thoughts & Messages

Guest Name

Thoughts & Messages

_____

_____

_____

_____

_____

_____

_____

EMAIL/PHONE

Guest Name

Thoughts & Messages

Guest Name

Thoughts & Messages

_____

_____

_____

_____

_____

_____

_____

EMAIL/PHONE

Guest Name

Thoughts & Messages

EMAIL/PHONE

Guest Name

Thoughts & Messages

Email/Phone

Guest Name

Thoughts & Messages

Email/Phone

Guest Name

Thoughts & Messages

_____

_____

_____

_____

_____

_____

_____

Email/Phone

Guest Name

Thoughts & Messages

EMAIL/PHONE

Guest Name

Thoughts & Messages

Email/Phone

Guest Name

Thoughts & Messages

_____

_____

_____

_____

_____

_____

_____

EMAIL/PHONE

Guest Name

Thoughts & Messages

_____

_____

_____

_____

_____

_____

_____

Email/Phone

Guest Name

Thoughts & Messages

_____

_____

_____

_____

_____

_____

EMAIL/PHONE

Guest Name

Thoughts & Messages

Email/Phone

Guest Name

Thoughts & Messages

Email/Phone

Guest Name

Thoughts & Messages

Email/Phone

Guest Name

_____

Thoughts & Messages

_____

_____

_____

_____

_____

_____

_____

EMAIL/PHONE

GIFT LOG

Name / Email / Phone	Gift

GIFT LOG

Name /Email /Phone	Gift

GIFT LOG

Name / Email / Phone	Gift

GIFT LOG

Name /Email /Phone	Gift

GIFT LOG

Name /Email /Phone	Gift

GIFT LOG

Name / Email / Phone	Gift

GIFT LOG

Name / Email / Phone	*Gift*

GIFT LOG

Name / Email / Phone	Gift

GIFT LOG

Name / Email / Phone	Gift

GIFT LOG

Name / Email / Phone	Gift

Made in the USA
Monee, IL
08 May 2023